Dramaline Publications
36-851 Palm View Road
Rancho Mirage, CA 92270
Phone 760/770-6076 Fax 760/770-4507
Website: dramaline.com Email: drama.line@gte.net

Cover art, Katie Gaon, age 7

This book is printed on 55# Glatfelter acid-free paper, a paper that meets the requirements of the American Standard of Permanence of paper for printed library material.

CONTENTS

GIRL/GIRL:

LISA & NANCY

A serious discussion regarding Halloween costumes.

LISA: I think I'm going as a witch.

NANCY: You can't.

LISA: Why?

NANCY: Because *I'm* going as a witch.

LISA: You can't! I've got a whole new witch outfit. A witch mask, a big pointed hat, a black cape, this real long wand—everything. I look real witchy.

NANCY: My mother made my outfit. I'll bet it's neater than yours anytime.

LISA: It is not!

NANCY: It's a whole lot scarier than the ones you go out and buy. We looked at the ones in the stores and they were dorky. You won't scare anyone.

LISA: My witch is scary. Scarier than yours any day. I put it on last night and jumped out from behind the porch at my brother and scared him so bad he got sick and had to sleep with his light on.

NANCY: My mom made me this long nose and stringy hair and she taught me how to cackle like a witch. (*She cackles.*)

LISA: You sound more like a chicken than a witch.

NANCY: Oh yeah? How do you know what a witch sounds like?

LISA: 'Cause I saw one in this movie one time—*Snow White.* She cackled like this— (*She cackles.*)

NANCY: That's a stupid cackle.

LISA: Oh yeah? You're just mad 'cause my cackle's better than yours.

NANCY: It is not!

LISA: You don't know anything about witches.

NANCY: They put spells on people.

LISA: And turn people into stuff, and fly on broomsticks, and keep bats around for pets.

NANCY: My mom made me a paper bat, too.

LISA: And mine bought me a big stuffed cat that lights up with green eyes and makes weird noises. (*She makes cat noises.*)

NANCY: You sound more like you're sick than like a cat.

LISA: I do not!

NANCY: You do, too!

LISA: Well—I'll still be a better witch than you.

NANCY: I'll bet I'll get twice as much stuff when we Trick or Treat than you do.

LISA: That's 'cause you'll have a bigger bag, that's why. Greedy!

NANCY: No—that's because I'll be a better witch. (*Pause.*) Hey! I have an idea. I'll be a witch this year, and you be a witch next year.

LISA: No way, José! How about you being a big mouse? You've got the face for it.

NANCY: Well—at least I'm won't look like a nerd in some stupid homemade witch outfit.

LISA: I'm not speaking to you anymore.

NANCY: Me, either. Not till after Halloween's over, anyhow.

CINDY & DORIS

The girls disagree with parental tastes when it comes to their clothes.

CINDY: So like we go on over to Newman's Department Store and Mom picks me out a whole bunch of stuff that you wouldn't want to go out of the house in, okay?

DORIS: Parents think we're like these old people, or something. Like we're fifteen or sixteen, you know. You should see the dress I got for my birthday. It's kinda like something you see in the old movies on TV when people had funny hair and wore shoes that looked like bricks strapped to their feet.

CINDY: I have to wear my new outfit when we go over to Aunt Ruth's this weekend. And my cousin Diane will be there and she always looks cool because my Aunt Ruth doesn't dress her stupid.

DORIS: Wow!

CINDY: I'll look like a monkey or something.

DORIS: It'll be neat when we're old enough to dress ourselves—

CINDY: Yeah.

DORIS: —and pick out clothes that other kids are wearing instead of old-timey junk that looks like you got it out of bags in some alley someplace.

CINDY: I had on my neat sneakers yesterday but I had to take them off because my grandmother was coming over. I hate leather shoes.

CINDY: Me, too.

DORIS: If you don't dress right, people look at you funny.

CINDY: Yeah. Like Thelma Feinstein.

DORIS: Yuck!

CINDY: Her mother must shop in outer space.

DORIS: I feel sorry for her. Always all dressed up real neat all the time. She looks like she'll break if she bends over.

CINDY: I asked her is she was hot in that stuff, and she said she was and that she's always real sweaty and has to take two showers a day.

DORIS: Two? Wow! One's bad enough.

CINDY: I don't think parents know anything about style and what looks good.

DORIS: If they did, they wouldn't dress like they do.

CINDY: You think getting old means you turn into a dork?

DORIS: I think it means you work all the time and complain and argue a lot.

CINDY: And yell at your kids for nothing and make them dress dumb.

DORIS: I picked out this really neat orange and blue sweat shirt with like balloons on it, you know. And Mom said it looked like a clown outfit. And here she was standing there in this ugly black dress with pearls and stuff.

CINDY: Moms are okay when it comes to cooking and like that but kind of lame when it comes to clothes. I wish they'd let us pick our own stuff.

DORIS: Yeah. 'Cause if you're not dressed right—forget it.

BETTY & MOLLY

Visiting the dentist is a "pain."

BETTY: My mom makes me go to the dentist twice a year.

MOLLY: Mine, too. And I have to brush my teeth twice every day, even when I don't eat much.

BETTY: Same here. Mom says going to the dentist every now and then and brushing every day keeps you from losing your teeth when you grow up and having crummy gums and looking like an old person when you're still young.

MOLLY: And to keep from having a great big mouth full of teeth that are all yellow and yucky.

BETTY: Yeah. And to keep you from having bad breath.

MOLLY: Like Billy Kramer's. His breath smells like my dog's. (*Pause.*) You know, we're really lucky we don't have to wear braces.

BETTY: I know. 'Cause our teeth are straight. Some kids have these teeth that stick out in front. (*She forces her upper teeth from her mouth in a bucked manner.*)

MOLLY: Braces are really awful.

BETTY: And they put rubber bands on them sometimes, too.

MOLLY: And food gets in them and it's enough to make you barf. (*She shivers.*)

BETTY: A lot of grownups wear braces, too. Like Virginia Fry's mother. She looks like she's got a mouth full of spoons.

MOLLY: I hate my dentist, Dr. Williams. He's always smiling and kidding around and trying to act friendly and he lets you run his chair up and down, but you know underneath he loves to hurt little kids.

BETTY: They all do. If they didn't, they wouldn't be dentists in the first place—they'd be regular people with real jobs.

MOLLY: They always tell you it's going to hurt them more than it is you and that there's nothing to be afraid of.

BETTY: Yeah. Sure.

MOLLY: That's before they start to stick junk in your mouth and mess around and poke you with these big things that look like stuff my dad has in his tool chest.

BETTY: Maybe if people were lucky they wouldn't have any teeth at all.

MOLLY: But how would you eat?

BETTY: Babies don't have teeth, and they get along okay.

MOLLY: But all they eat is soft stuff.

BETTY: So? You could live on like candy and ice cream and pie and cake and frozen yogurt—stuff like that.

MOLLY: But you'd turn into a blimp.

BETTY: Maybe—but you'd never ever have to worry about going to the dentist as long as you live.

KRISTIN & JANICE

The girls uncover an old adage, "Beauty is only skin deep."

KRISTIN: Do you think Corky Johnson is cute?
JANICE: Corky Johnson? Oooooh! He isn't cute, he's gross.
KRISTIN: He is not.
JANICE: I saw him the other day and he was wearing ugly shoes. He was with Eddie Clark.
KRISTIN: Eddie Clark? Oooooh!
JANICE: Eddie Clark is cute.
KRISTIN: No way. He's got these ears that stick way out and make him look like a donkey.
JANICE: He does not. He has nice ears. And good manners. He opened the door for me one time.
KRISTIN: Every time I look at him I almost laugh.
JANICE: That's not nice. Making fun of people isn't nice.
KRISTIN: But he looks like Dumbo. (*She pulls out her ears.*)
JANICE: Stop that! You don't see me making fun of Corky Johnson even though he's got a neck that's too long. (*She extends her neck.*)
KRISTIN: I thought you said it wasn't nice to make fun of people.
JANICE: Can I help it if his neck is funny?
KRISTIN: Nobody's perfect.
JANICE: How about Frank MacKenzie?
KRISTIN: Frank MacKenzie?
JANICE: His father owns the MacKenzie Lumber Company.
KRISTIN: He's really cute.
JANICE: He's perfect.
KRISTIN: He's too tall to be perfect.
JANICE: But he's really cute.

KRISTIN: He's like this bean pole and it makes you feel funny when you stand next to him, like you're this dwarf or something.

JANICE: But he's nice looking and dresses cool. That's because his dad owns a lumber company.

KRISTIN: Corky Johnson's dad owns a drug store.

JANICE: Corky Johnson. Oooooh!

KRISTIN: You know, sometimes it's hard to know when people are cute, you know.

JANICE: Yeah.

KRISTIN: Because sometimes people aren't cute but they're nice and it makes them okay.

JANICE: Like Harry Gerber. He's got everything wrong with him.

KRISTIN: Wow—Harry Gerber. His glasses are so thick they make his eyes look like a fish's. And his clothes are awful. His father is dead. His mom works at the dry cleaners.

JANICE: But he's nice.

KRISTIN: Yeah, even though he isn't cute, he's nice—to everybody.

JANICE: And he's nice to be around.

KRISTIN: I wonder why?

JANICE: I dunno.

KRISTIN: Maybe being cute isn't everything, you know.

JANICE: Yeah. Like maybe it's nothing.

ERIN & MEGAN

The girls are aware of the dangers of prejudice.

ERIN: There IS a whole bunch of new kids coming into school lately.

MEGAN: Yeah, from all over.

ERIN: It seems like nobody's from around here anymore. Nobody, you know.

MEGAN: Last year I knew everybody because most of the kids were from the neighborhood.

ERIN: Now I feel like everyone's a stranger.

MEGAN: My dad says it's a good thing we get kids from all kinds of different places.

ERIN: So does my mom.

MEGAN: He says this way we get to know about people who are different from us, about how they act and think and feel and stuff.

ERIN: There's some pretty weird kids in my classes.

MEGAN: Maybe they think you're weird, too.

ERIN: I'm not weird!

MEGAN: I know. What I meant was, to them—the kids who seem different, I mean—to them you might seem weird because of the way you dress and act and the things you believe in and stuff.

ERIN: When to me it isn't weird at all? Because this is like me and it's all I know. Right?

MEGAN: Yeah, like that.

ERIN: I never thought of it like that. Maybe other kids think I'm the one who's off the wall.

MEGAN: Or far out. When you really aren't, you know. You're just like . . . like you.

ERIN: It's kind of hard to see people who are different and not think they're weird.

MEGAN: Yeah. Like when I first saw Melody White. I though she was a real freak. But after I got to know her, she was okay.

ERIN: Most kids are okay, I guess. I mean—like they're pretty nice. I mean, you know—

MEGAN: I know. I think that, too. How kids and grown-up people—when you get to know them, that is—how they're pretty much alike.

ERIN: My sister—she's in high school—says there are all kinds of different kids in her classes.

MEGAN: Does she think they're okay?

ERIN: She does. And she says the same thing—that all people are pretty much the same. She even wrote this poem about it for her English class.

MEGAN: I hate poems.

ERIN: Me, too. But this one's okay. I even liked it so much I remembered it. Wanna hear it?

MEGAN: I guess so.

ERIN: It's called "Opposites." (*She clears her throat before reciting.*)

> Opposites are both the same
> Divided only by a name,
> A name that often separates
> And causes fears and causes hates.
> But we are one, both you and I
> I know your sadness when you cry,
> And I know your gladness when you laugh,
> 'Cause I was born your other half.

MINDY & AMY

Brothers often seem to be alien creatures.

MINDY: Last night, right when I was getting ready for bed, Roger, my little pig of a brother, came in my room and threw water on me.

AMY: My brother, Alan, he does stuff like that, too. All the time. And my mom never spanks him or anything. But if I do something to him that's not even half as bad, I always get it good. That's because he's a little baby who cries if you even look at him.

MINDY: That's because boys are their favorites.

AMY: Alan put chewing gum in my doll's hair, and when I told Mom, she said I shouldn't leave my doll out where Alan can find it.

MINDY: All my brothers are all the time doing bad stuff to me. Like beating me up and pushing me around and not letting me watch my favorite TV shows.

AMY: Boys are creeps.

MINDY: Even my big older brother who's in high school. He doesn't treat me mean, he just acts like I'm not even around, which is worse. I can be right in the same room with him and he never says anything to me. I wish he'd yell at me, or something.

AMY: Yeah, that way you'd know—even though you know he hates you—that he doesn't think you're a total nothing.

MINDY: If I had anything to do with it, my mom and dad would only have girls.

AMY: Girls can be jerks, too, but at least they don't beat you around and play rough and get into your things and act like major weasels.

MINDY: My big sister thinks boys are pigs, too. I hear her on the phone with her boyfriend and she calls him a dork a lot. He must be, because he always calls right back so she can call him a dork and hang up on him again.

AMY: I like anything better than boys.

MINDY: When I grow up, I'm never going out with boys.

AMY: Me, either.

MINDY: I'm just going to stay home and watch videos and eat junk.

AMY: Me, too. Watching videos and eating junk is the neatest thing a person can do. That and shopping and hanging around the house listening to your mom and dad argue.

MINDY: Would you ever go on a date with a boy?

AMY: No way, José.

MINDY: Me either.

AMY: I hate boys. All of them. (*Pause.*) Except, maybe for David Clingman.

MINDY: And Dick Lawrence.

AMY: Yeah, they're cute.

MINDY: If they're cute—even though you hate them— sometimes boys can be kinda okay.

KAREN & KATY

Being the new kid on the block carries many social difficulties.

KAREN: Hi. You're the new kid who just moved in, aren't you?

KATY: Yes.

KAREN: Into the big white house on the corner.

KATY: Yes.

KAREN: That used to be Mary Smith's house.

KATY: I guess. I don't know. I don't know anything about this neighborhood.

KAREN: Mary was my best friend. She had to move because her dad got this job up in Chicago. We used to play together all the time and she used to sleep over and everything.

KATY: That's nice.

KAREN: She was really pretty. Prettier than anyone. She had lots of friends.

KATY: I used to have lots of friends, too. Back in Detroit. I had more friends than anyone. But now—since moving here—I don't know anybody.

KAREN: Which room do you have?

KATY: Huh?

KAREN: Which one is your room? You know, in your house?

KATY: Oh. It's the glassed-in one over the porch in the back.

KAREN: That was Mary's room, too. She had it full of all kinds of neat stuff. I used to play in her room a lot. I wish she hadn't had to leave. I really miss her. She was a good friend.

KATY: I miss my friends, too. You think I don't? Hey, at least you're still at home where you know people and kids and everyone in your school.

KAREN: Hey! You'll get to know them too, after a while.

KATY: I dunno. The kids around here aren't very friendly.

KAREN: Yes they are.

KATY: They are not. They're all just like you. I've seen you lots of times, and this is the first time you've ever spoken to me.

KAREN: That's because you're the one who isn't friendly.

KATY: I am too!

KAREN: You're the one who always runs inside every time I come by.

KATY: So?

KAREN: So maybe you don't have friends because you really aren't trying to; ever think of that?

KATY: You haven't got any idea what it's like being a stranger. And just because you're new, the kids around here treat you like you're from another planet, or something. I don't want to be friends with any of the jerks in this neighborhood. I don't care if they like me or not.

KAREN: Okay then. I gotta go. (*She turns to leave.*)

KATY: Where you going?

KAREN: Home.

KATY: Wait a minute! You wanna come to my place first and see my room?

MARIA & DARLENE

Their mother's passing has altered the lives of sisters.

MARIA: I'll run away before I go stay with a bunch of strangers.

DARLENE: You have to. And besides, Aunt Ethel isn't a stranger.

MARIA: I'd rather die than live with Aunt Ethel.

DARLENE: C'mon, she's nice.

MARIA: I'm not going to live with her I said!

DARLENE: But Daddy can't take care of us right now.

MARIA: He doesn't want to, you mean. He doesn't even care.

DARLENE: He does, too. Don't say that. I know he does. He just wants us to move in with Aunt Ethel for a little while, that's all, until he like figures stuff out, okay?

MARIA: Why did Mom have to go and die, anyway?

DARLENE: I don't know.

MARIA: Why does anyone have to die?

DARLENE: They just do, that's all, everybody—you and me someday, too.

MARIA: Why'd she have to go and die and leave us alone? (*She sobs.*) I hate her for dying, I hate her!

DARLENE: Take that back!

MARIA: I'm not taking anything back—I hate her for leaving us. It's all her fault. And now—now Daddy's leaving us, too.

DARLENE: No. He isn't!

MARIA: He is!

DARLENE: Gimme a break, okay? Like it isn't anyone's fault. And you can't go blaming Mom for dying, either. That's not right. That's crazy.

MARIA: But if she were alive, we wouldn't have to go live with Aunt Ethel 'cause she'd be here to take care of us and Daddy would be nice and everything would be okay like always.

DARLENE: But things aren't like always, all right? So we have to go. We can't hang around here.

MARIA: So why not? So why can't we? This is our home, isn't it?

DARLENE: But there won't be anyone around. Daddy has to work. He has to travel. He can't just go off and leave us here all by ourselves. Little kids can't stay by themselves.

MARIA: Oh yeah, why? Who says? You, just 'cause you're two years older? Big deal.

DARLENE: Everybody knows that kids shouldn't be left alone. Daddy's doing this because he loves us.

MARIA: If he did, he wouldn't make us go away.

DARLENE: Just till he changes his job. Then we'll all be back together. It won't be long, he promised.

MARIA: I miss Mom so much.

DARLENE: Me, too.

MARIA: I want her back. Why can't she come back?

DARLENE: Because she's dead, that's why. But Daddy's alive; that's the most important thing. And so are we.

MARY & LINDA

Their room is a special place.

MARY: You can come on over to my place if you want to and hang around and we can have Cokes and stuff—
LINDA: I don't want to.
MARY: —and watch TV and play with my dolls.
LINDA: No, you can come to my house for a change.
MARY: I always come to your house.
LINDA: No way. And besides, I've got more stuff to play with than you.
MARY: Since when?
LINDA: Since always.
MARY: And my room is special.
LINDA: Mine, too.
MARY: I've got secret stuff that nobody knows about, not even my mom even—nobody.
LINDA: I keep my special stuff in a place where nobody could find it in a million years.
MARY: Where?
LINDA: If I told you, it wouldn't be secret.
MARY: I'll tell you where my stuff is hidden if you tell me where you keep yours.
LINDA: I don't want to.
MARY: We're like best friends, aren't we?
LINDA: Yeah, but—
MARY: And do everything together and go everywhere together. So why shouldn't we know about each other's secret places?

LINDA: Because my room is special, that's why. It's like where I go to be alone and do neat stuff and not have to be anybody but me.

MARY: Yeah. You mean, like when you get yelled at and mess up in school and everything is bad. Then you can go to your room and nobody can hurt you and nothing can go wrong.

LINDA: Where you have secret stuff you keep in secret places where only you know where it's at. That's the reason I won't tell anyone where it is—not even you, and you're my best friend. 'Cause if I did, it would be like giving up something that makes me only me.

MARY: My favorite time in my room is at night when I can lie in bed and look around and know that nothing can get me. And when it rains and I can stay in and play with my dolls and draw and color.

LINDA: And pretend.

MARY: You can pretend in your room more than anywhere else.

LINDA: Do you talk to your dolls?

MARY: Sometimes.

LINDA: I do. A lot. And they talk to me, too. And they say anything I want them to.

MARY: Do you tell them where your secret stuff is hidden?

LINDA: Uh huh.

MARY: Well—if you tell them, why won't you tell me?

LINDA: Because dolls are better than people when it comes to keeping secrets.

BETSY & SHIRLEY

Naming your pet can be a serious matter.

BETSY: Last Saturday we went down to the animal pound and picked out this real cute dog. He's kind of dopey and ratty looking, but he's super gentle and smart and nice and he doesn't mess up the rugs.

SHIRLEY: That's where we got Harold, our cat.

BETSY: Harold?

SHIRLEY: My dad named him. After my uncle, because he said he looks like him—shifty and weird around the eyes.

BETSY: We haven't named our dog yet. But that's a good idea, naming him after some person you know, I mean.

SHIRLEY: Mom flipped when we walked in with Harold. She said he looked like a little wolf.

BETSY: Like your Uncle Harold?

SHIRLEY: Yeah, real sneaky.

BETSY: We have three dogs now.

SHIRLEY: Wow!

BETSY: And our bird, Chatters.

SHIRLEY: I'd like to have a bird, too. But Mom says if we bring a bird home, she'll cook it and eat it. She's had it with pets.

BETSY: Birds are really neat, but I feel sorry for them because they have to stay caged up all the time. If not, they'll fly off and you'll never see them again.

SHIRLEY: What are you going to name your new dog?

BETSY: I don't know.

SHIRLEY: Maybe after someone in your family, like we did Harold.

BETSY: I don't think we have anyone who looks like a dog.

SHIRLEY: I'll bet, if you think about it, you'll think of someone. What's your dog look like?

BETSY: Well, kind of short and fat and kind of dumpy with hair that smells funny. Hey, I know!—maybe Florence, after my aunt. She's short and fat and she puts this stuff on her hair that smells like the stuff you wax your floor with.

SHIRLEY: I like Florence. That's a good name.

BETSY: You don't think it's kind of lame?

SHIRLEY: No more lame than Harold. And it would make your aunt real happy.

BETSY: I dunno—to be named after something that's dumpy and fat and has hair that stinks?

SHIRLEY: My Uncle Harold thought it was neat that we named our cat after him. Every time he comes over, he brings along a can of Nine Lives.

BETSY: Wow, wait a minute, I almost forgot—Florence is no good.

SHIRLEY: How come?

BETSY: Because it's a boy dog, that's why.

SHIRLEY: So what? He won't know the difference.

BETSY: Yeah—but my Aunt Florence sure will.

BOY/BOY:

MIKE & ERIC

They discuss that eternal mystery—girls.

MIKE: Ya know what?

ERIC: What?

MIKE: Sue Anne Miller keeps looking at me real funny all the time, and it gives me the creeps.

ERIC: Girls are supposed to give you the creeps.

MIKE: Sometimes she's got this real dopey look on her face like she's sick at the stomach, or something.

ERIC: Then don't look at her.

MIKE: You can't help it when she's staring at you all the time like with these big huge eyes that are all spacey and weird.

ERIC: That's because she likes you.

MIKE: No way. If she did, she'd act nice the next time I see her. Instead, she's always real rude and off the wall. If she likes me, how come she acts like a jerk?

ERIC: They always act like jerks if they like you.

MIKE: That's crazy.

ERIC: All girls are crazy. It they weren't, they wouldn't be girls.

MIKE: How do you know?

ERIC: 'Cause that's what my dad says. He says that girls and women are okay but that they're different and sometimes they can make you goofy.

MIKE: Yeah, they can. Like Sue Ann Miller looking at me with this stupid smile on her face. She's making me goofy, I think. 'Cause when I look back at her, I get this creepy feeling in my stomach like I just ate too much.

ERIC: That's because you like her.

MIKE: Sue Ann Miller? I hate Sue Ann Miller more than anything.

ERIC: I used to think I hated Janet Moore, too. Because she was always coming up to me and smiling and making me feel like a toad. But after a while, after I got over feeling weird, I got to like her and now when she looks at me I feel more like a lion than a toad.

MIKE: That's crazy.

ERIC: What do you feel like when Sue Ann stares at you?

MIKE: Awful.

ERIC: I mean—like what kind of animal?

MIKE: I dunno—a pig, maybe.

ERIC: That's because you like her.

MIKE: Because I feel like a pig?

ERIC: That's the way you're supposed to feel. Crummy. That means you like her.

MIKE: I hate her. She's always looking at me like I'm a chocolate sundae, or something.

ERIC: She makes you feel like a chocolate sundae?

MIKE: No way. More like a big hunk of cheese.

ERIC: That's good, because cheese stinks.

MIKE: So does Sue Ann Miller.

ANDY & RALPH

Life's realities can have a sobering effect.

ANDY: Where you going?

RALPH: Over to Jimmy Gomez's house.

ANDY: How come?

RALPH: Because he's sick.

ANDY: You don't ever come over to see me when I'm sick.

RALPH: That's because when you're sick, it's just colds and the stomachache and dumb stuff like that. But Jimmy's bad sick.

ANDY: Like he's got the flu, or something?

RALPH: Worse that that.

ANDY: Nothing's worse than the flu. I had it last winter and I had to stay home from school for two whole weeks.

RALPH: He's got like this thing wrong with his blood. Where bad things are happening and making him weak and tired.

ANDY: Gee, that's the pits.

RALPH: Yeah, and like my mom says, he may not ever get any better.

ANDY: You mean, be sick for the rest of his life?

RALPH: Worse.

ANDY: How can anything be worse than being sick every day? I can't stand being sick for an hour even.

RALPH: He's going to die.

ANDY: Jimmy Gomez?

RALPH: That's what Mom says.

ANDY: Wow. I didn't know kids died. I thought you had to get old first.

RALPH: I guess when you've got something wrong they can't fix, you can die—anytime.

ANDY: Have you seen him?

RALPH: Yeah, last Saturday.

ANDY: Yeah—?

RALPH: He doesn't look so good. He's real skinny and pale and when he talks, his voice is so weak it doesn't sound like him talking anymore.

ANDY: Is he afraid?

RALPH: I don't think so.

ANDY: Boy, I'd be for sure if I knew I was going to die.

RALPH: You wanna come along?

ANDY: No way! Forget it!

RALPH: It's not so bad. Honest.

ANDY: Yeah, sure.

RALPH: Even though he's sick, he's still funny. You remember how funny he always was, don't you? Well, he's still like that. Real funny and laughing, even though he knows he's going to die.

ANDY: He knows it? He knows he's going to die?

RALPH: That's what my mom says. But you'd never ever know it, 'cause he never lets on. He's super brave and never complains. He's really a neat guy. I'm gonna miss him.

ANDY: You know what?

RALPH: What?

ANDY: Maybe I will come along after all.

ERNIE & BOBBY

When it comes to food, nutrition is not a major factor.

ERNIE: So Mom says, "Ernie, eat all your Brussels sprouts."

BOBBY: Brussels sprouts? Wow!

ERNIE: But I can't, no way.

BOBBY: They taste like when you fall down and get grass in your mouth. Yuck.

ERNIE: So she makes me sit there till I eat 'em, okay? Till I eat these things that even my dog won't eat. I tried to feed him some and he spit 'em out and went crazy like he does when I turn up the stereo too high.

BOBBY: Animals are too smart to eat junk like that. They go for meat and stuff. Our cats like birds.

ERNIE: I didn't know what to do, you know. I mean, like I could never eat a plate full of Brussels sprouts in a million years.

BOBBY: So what'd you do?

ERNIE: I kicked off my shoes under the table, and while Mom wasn't looking, I stuffed the Brussels sprouts into them.

BOBBY: Hey, neat. I'll have to remember that.

ERNIE: Then I acted like I was eating the last one by making my mouth move with my tongue in my cheek, like this. (*He shoves his tongue into the side of his mouth, creating a large, round protuberance, and chews.*) This way, she thought I was chewing on a Brussels sprout. The hard thing was sneaking my shoes away so she wouldn't see me.

BOBBY: They always make you eat dumb stuff. Stuff like carrots, and beets, and spinach.

ERNIE: They think it's cool for you to eat slop.

BOBBY: The last time I ate spinach I threw up.

ERNIE: Hey, it's better than keeping that junk in your stomach—a bunch of slimy green stuff that looks gross on your plate. And they try to tell you it's healthy for you—
BOBBY: Yeah. Boy.
ERNIE: —that it's got all kinds of vitamins in it that make you strong.
BOBBY: I never feel strong after I throw up. I feel weak and weird and have sort of a headache.
ERNIE: My folks like salads.
BOBBY: Mine, too.
ERNIE: They sit around eating them and expect you to eat them, too.
BOBBY: Why would anybody wanna eat a salad when he can have a Big Mac and fries?
ERNIE: Or a chocolate shake?
BOBBY: Know what? I'll bet they don't like salads, either. I'll bet they just act like they do to get you to eat them. Like they do with little babies to get them to eat this ugly strained food.
ERNIE: I never ever thought of that.
BOBBY: I'll bet they never swallow their salads. I'll bet they go someplace and spit 'em out.
ERNIE: Yeah.
BOBBY: Or maybe, while you're not looking, they stuff 'em into their shoes.

CHARLES & BRIAN

The act of bathing is one of last resort.

CHARLES: Boy—you smell funny, you know that?

BRIAN: That's 'cause I just had to take a shower.

CHARLES: With what? You smell weird.

BRIAN: I'll smell like this for a while, till the soap wears off. I always smell funny for a while when I'm clean. So do you, you turkey!

CHARLES: No way.

BRIAN: Oh yeah? I've smelled you before and you smell worse than I do anytime—

CHARLES: I do not.

BRIAN: —like you just took a bath in perfume, or something.

CHARLES: We use Ivory at our house. And Ivory doesn't smell. It just floats.

BRIAN: Then how come you smell like my aunt when she comes over to visit on Sundays? Or my sister when she goes out with some dude?

CHARLES: At least I don't smell like the stuff my mom sprays around the room to get rid of bad odors.

BRIAN: It must be the shampoo.

CHARLES: Ooh, you had to get your hair washed, too?

BRIAN: Creeps. It's bad enough to have to take a shower. Then they go and rub a bunch of shampoo into your hair.

CHARLES: And it always gets in your eyes.

BRIAN: I hate getting my face wet.

CHARLES: Why can't we just slick down our hair with some grease, or something?

BRIAN: My dad and mom take a shower every day.

CHARLES: Mine, too.

BRIAN: It's like they like it. My dad even sings while he's doing it and wakes everybody up.

CHARLES: How come older people like to do all the things that kids hate?

BRIAN: Just to be rats, I think. Maybe that's the good thing about being a grownup. You can be a rat and get away with it.

CHARLES: But why would anybody want to get all wet if they don't have to? Especially when it's cold. (*He shivers.*)

BRIAN: I don't get dirty all over, anyhow.

CHARLES: Yeah. If nobody can see it, what's the difference? Like scrubbing the bottoms of your feet.

BRIAN: And washing behind your ears. People don't go around looking behind your ears anyway.

CHARLES: Not unless they're some kind of nerd. Taking a bath all the time doesn't make any sense. It's just this big dumb thing they make you do because you're little and they can get away with it.

BRIAN: When I grow up, I'm never taking a bath or a shower.

CHARLES: Me, either. I'll just go for a swim once in a while.

BRIAN: That way you won't have to use soap.

CHARLES: Yeah. And run around smelling like a bunch of stale flowers all the time.

TEDDY & DANNY

Nothing is worse than being out of step with the latest trends.

TEDDY: Wow!

DANNY: What's wrong?

TEDDY: Your hair. Far out, dude.

DANNY: My older sister cut it.

TEDDY: Neat.

DANNY: She's kind of a spaz most of the time, but when it comes to hair, she's okay. She went to this big beauty place when they teach you to do all this neat far-out hair stuff.

TEDDY: What do you call it?

DANNY: I don't think there's a name for it.

TEDDY: Maybe a Mohawk?

DANNY: I don't know.

TEDDY: It kind of reminds me of like when dogs get bad fur and they cut hunks out of it so whatever they have won't spread and mess them up.

DANNY: You think I look like a dog?

TEDDY: Yeah, kind of, but it still looks okay because it's really cool and different. Boy, if I ever got my hair cut like that, I'd get yelled at good.

DANNY: My mom isn't speaking to my sister.

TEDDY: She doesn't like it?

DANNY: She says I look like a skinned rat.

TEDDY: You do look kinda like a skinned rat, I guess, come to think of it.

DANNY: I do not!

TEDDY: You do.

DANNY: Thanks a lot.

TEDDY: I mean, you know, I mean like a skinned rat kind of but still cool because you look like someone on MTV.

DANNY: I do? Who?

TEDDY: I don't know, lots of people. I see a whole bunch of people on MTV with these kinds of haircuts and clothes that are falling off because they have so many rips and tears.

DANNY: Every time my jeans get cool tears, my mom dumps them in the trash.

TEDDY: Mine, too. Just when they're getting to look good. What'd your dad say about your haircut?

DANNY: He isn't speaking to my sister, either.

TEDDY: At least your sister's getting all the blame.

DANNY: Yeah, that's the best part.

TEDDY: But I don't have a sister. If I ever got my hair cut like that, I'd get all the blame because it'd be my idea.

DANNY: You should let my sister cut yours, too.

TEDDY: Forget it. You want me to get killed?

DANNY: But that way you can say she goofed up.

TEDDY: You mean, like her scissors slipped, or something?

DANNY: Yeah, and that way they won't be able to blame it on you because it won't be your fault. I mean, you just went in for a regular haircut, okay?

TEDDY: Hey, yeah, neat. And then I'll look cool like a skinned rat, too.

MICHAEL & CALVIN

Competition starts at an early age.

MICHAEL: What'd you get on your home project?
CALVIN: An "A".
MICHAEL: Ms. Moore gave you an "A"?
CALVIN: Yep.
MICHAEL: An "A" for a bunch of stupid leaves painted different colors? No way!
CALVIN: Wanna bet? She wrote a big "A" right across the bottom of it. What'd you get?
MICHAEL: I don't remember.
CALVIN: Yes, you do.
MICHAEL: Forget it.
CALVIN: C'mon.
MICHAEL: Forget it, okay?
CALVIN: I'll bet you got a lame grade.
MICHAEL: Well, at least my mom didn't help me with mine!
CALVIN: Who says?
MICHAEL: Everybody.
CALVIN: No way!
MICHAEL: Because your project looked too good to be done by a kid. You cheated.
CALVIN: I did not!
MICHAEL: (*Chants.*) Cheaters never win! Cheaters never win!
CALVIN: Shut up, goon!
MICHAEL: My project was as good as yours any day and I go and get a "C". But at least mine was fair.

CALVIN: You got a "C" because your project looked like junk, that's why. I saw it. It was stupid. All the kids were laughing at it.

MICHAEL: They were not!

CALVIN: Marcy Goldberg said it looked like someone had sat in the middle of a chocolate cake.

MICHAEL: Marcy Goldberg's a big fat jerk!

CALVIN: You're just mad because I got a better grade than you, that's what.

MICHAEL: Cheater!

CALVIN: That's the reason you took your project home right away instead of leaving it in the room like the rest of the kids. Because you didn't want anybody to know you got a bad grade because your project stunk.

MICHAEL: (*Sings.*) Cheaters never win! Cheaters never win!

CALVIN: You're a pig, you know that? And I was going to let you see a bunch of my new videos, too.

MICHAEL: You were?

CALVIN: Before you called me a cheater, that is.

MICHAEL: Hey, I was only kidding, you know. I mean— give me a break.

CALVIN: Then take back I was cheating.

MICHAEL: Okay, okay. Lighten up. I was only kidding. I take it back. I'm sorry.

CALVIN: You know what, Michael? Sometimes you don't act like you're my best friend.

ADAM & BILLY

Brothers discuss their social station.

ADAM: I was over to Jimmy Montez's house and he was home all by himself.
BILLY: How come?
ADAM: 'Cause she has to work.
BILLY: I'm glad our mom doesn't have to work.
ADAM: His sister takes care of him and sometimes his grandmother, but a lot of times he has to hang around by himself.
BILLY: How come his dad isn't there?
ADAM: Because he lives someplace else.
BILLY: Just like Eric Mills. His dad lives someplace else, too. And he only gets to see him once in a while instead of every day like we do our dad.
ADAM: Jimmy's dad lives in another city.
BILLY: Wow!
ADAM: And he only gets to see him like during the summer and on holidays and stuff.
BILLY: I don't think it'd be any fun having your mom and dad not living together. I mean, it'd be like it wouldn't be a family, you know. It'd be like it wouldn't be anything anymore because your mom and dad wouldn't be in the same house.
ADAM: Jimmy said his dad and mom don't like each other anymore.
BILLY: Gee.
ADAM: They don't even speak anymore, and when his dad picks him up, he just honks his horn out front.
BILLY: That's too bad, you know.

ADAM: Yeah. Not speaking gives me the creeps. I don't know how people can go around not talking to each other.
BILLY: I guess you have to be real mad.
ADAM: I wouldn't know what to do if Dad wasn't around.
BILLY: Me, either.
ADAM: The best thing is when he comes home at night and we have dinner and all sit and talk and watch TV and mess around.
BILLY: I never want to move. I hope we stay here forever. And I hope Mom and Dad don't ever get so mad at each other that they don't live together.
ADAM: Jimmy stays in a lot—in his room.
BILLY: How come?
ADAM: He doesn't like to leave because he said he's afraid if he does, something will happen to him.
BILLY: Like what?
ADAM: I dunno. Something bad. He says as long as he hangs around the house, he feels okay. He says he has all these real weird dreams anymore, too.
BILLY: I wonder how come a lot of people don't get along so good after they get married?
ADAM: I don't think a lot people should get married in the first place.
BILLY: Yeah.
ADAM: That way, if they goof up, it doesn't make any difference.
BILLY: And it doesn't mess up little kids.
ADAM: (*After a pause.*) You know, sometimes I don't think older people are very smart.

ROGER & BEN

The boys disagree regarding diet.

ROGER: Wow!

BEN: What's wrong?

ROGER: How can you eat that junk?

BEN: Who says it's junk?

ROGER: Everybody knows that hot dogs are junk. People shouldn't eat stuff like that.

BEN: How about you? You eat all kinds of stuff. I've seen you.

ROGER: No way!

BEN: The other day, while we watched videos, you ate a whole pizza.

ROGER: Yeah, that may be, but pizza isn't as bad for you as hot dogs and burgers and fries and stuff like that.

BEN: Fries are okay. Especially McDonald's.

ROGER: McDonald's food is greasy barf. All that kind of stuff is.

BEN: You just don't know what's good, that's all.

ROGER: My sister says hot dogs and burgers are bad for you because they've got a bunch of fat in them.

BEN: What does she know?

ROGER: Julie knows a lot, that's what.

BEN: If she knows so much about food, how come she's big as a blimp?

ROGER: Don't go calling my sister a blimp, okay?

BEN: Everybody else does.

ROGER: They do not!

BEN: She looks like one of those big balloons on the Thanksgiving Day Parade on TV.

ROGER: You'd better be careful what you say about my sister. What about your brother? He's fatter than Julie anytime. He's like this big huge whale I saw last summer when we were on vacation.

BEN: Yeah, but he doesn't go around telling people not to eat burgers and fries and stuff. He minds his own business. He's cool. He doesn't say anything.

ROGER: That's because he's always got his mouth stuffed full of food, that's why.

BEN: Well, I don't care what Julie says, I'm not going to stop eating burgers and dogs and Cokes and stuff. What does she eat, anyhow? A whole bunch of fat stuff, I'll bet. You don't get to be as big as a bus from drinking water.

ROGER: You'd better watch it, okay? Or I'll go home and tell Julie what you said about her.

BEN: So what?

ROGER: You'll be sorry, that's what. She'll get you good!

BEN: Oh yeah, what's she gonna do, come sit on me, pizza face?

JERRY & ROSS

Sports aren't for everyone.

JERRY: Hey! How come you never play baseball or football or anything?
ROSS: Playing ball is stupid.
JERRY: You're chicken.
ROSS: No way, ape brain!
JERRY: You're afraid of getting hurt, that's what.
ROSS: Who says?
JERRY: Everybody.
ROSS: Oh yeah?
JERRY: Yeah!
ROSS: Just because I don't like sports doesn't mean I'm afraid. Goon.
JERRY: Who you calling a goon?
ROSS: You see anyone else around here?
JERRY: For two cents I'd punch you out.
ROSS: Go ahead and try!
JERRY: Maybe I will!
ROSS: What you going to hit me with, a ballbat?
JERRY: What will *you* use, a book?
ROSS: So I like books, so what?
JERRY: That's the reason you don't have any friends.
ROSS: Because I like books?
JERRY: Yeah. Nobody likes people who read books all the time and don't play games and stuff.
ROSS: How many books have you read?
JERRY: I dunno. Who cares?
ROSS: (*Holds up a book.*) See this book?
JERRY: Yeah.

ROSS: It's all about how the Americans invaded France during World War II. It tells all kinds of neat stuff about how it was the biggest invasion of all time with the most tanks and planes and everything. And with like thousands of guys parachuting in so the sky was like almost black with them coming down.

JERRY: Wow!

ROSS: It tells about all kinds of battles and people and how the war was won.

JERRY: No kidding? I like planes. Like the old ones you see in the old movies.

ROSS: You mean like P-51s and Spitfires and that?

JERRY: Yeah, like that. Those were really neat planes with neat guys flying them. Heroes and aces. My dad knows a guy who flew a P-51.

ROSS: Wow! Really?

JERRY: Yeah. He's real old now. I've been in his basement where he keeps all kinds of neat stuff.

ROSS: Wow! I'd sure like to see that.

JERRY: You can come along with me sometime. If you want to, that is.

ROSS: Hey, that'd be neat. (*Pause.*) Say, maybe I'll play some ball with you guys tomorrow. Okay?

JERRY: Sure, okay. Say, er, ah—

ROSS: Yeah?

JERRY: like would you mind if I borrow that book sometime?

FRANK & MARK

The boys discuss the advantages of illness.

FRANK: I haven't seen you for a while.

MARK: I've been home. With the flu.

FRANK: Me, too.

MARK: No kidding? I was real sick and had to stay in bed for almost a week.

FRANK: I stayed in my room and watched TV and listened to my mom yell at my sister a lot.

MARK: I like it when my mom yells at my sister. She's a big goon. When you're sick, they don't yell at you as much. Ever notice that?

FRANK: Yeah. They treat you nice and wait on you and bring you all kinds of stuff that they won't let you have when you're well.

MARK: My aunt brought me over all these neat videos. And my mom baked me some chocolate-chip cookies. I ate them all up in one afternoon and got sicker than ever and everybody thought it was the flu but it wasn't.

FRANK: The only trouble with being sick is that they take you to the doctor and he pokes you and sticks this stick in your mouth that makes you choke.

MARK: Yeah. And they make you take all this crummy medicine that tastes so bad that you almost want to barf.

FRANK: My grandmother came over with this big can of grease and rubbed it all over my chest. It smelled so bad it made my eyes water.

MARK: Wow!

FRANK: She said she rubbed it on my dad when he was little and that it always made him feel better. When I asked Dad if the stuff worked, he didn't say anything—he just turned around and walked out of my room.

MARK: They always have a bunch of lame stuff like that that's supposed to make you feel a whole lot better that winds up making you feel a whole lot worse. They made me swallow this big glob of green ugly stuff that looked like runny Jell-O, or something. Yuck. Bad news.

FRANK: The worse it tastes, the better it's supposed to be, I guess.

MARK: I like to hang around the house, though. This way I don't have to go to school.

FRANK: Yeah. Hanging around is okay. Especially when you get to watch videos and read and lie around in bed all day while other kids are sitting in school listening to a bunch of lame junk. How are you feeling? Are you okay now?

MARK: Yeah, I feel okay.

FRANK: Me, too. But I'm kinda not acting like I feel so good, you know.

MARK: Yeah. 'Cause when you start acting normal, they start yelling at you right away again.

FRANK: You know, sometimes I think being sick is better than feeling good.

BOY/GIRL:

JANET & BILL

Brother and sister discuss vacation possibilities.

JANET: Where do you think we're going this year?
BILL: I dunno.
JANET: I heard mom talking to Aunt Sally about the Smoky Mountains.
BILL: Oh, wow! The Smoky Mountains is the pits.
JANET: We been there three times already.
BILL: It's pretty but real boring. There's nothing for kids to do. Except play around the hotel and watch people sleeping in their chairs.
JANET: And I hate watching those mountain people make those stupid wooden bowls and junk.
BILL: Yeah. And do weaving. Who cares about weaving, anyway?
JANET: Old people—they're into weaving a lot, I think. Grandma loves to watch them weave.
BILL: Yeah, old people like stupid junk like that.
JANET: The last time I got poison ivy, remember?
BILL: Yeah. You looked like an alligator.
JANET: I did not!
BILL: You were gross. (*He giggles.*)
JANET: It's not funny, lame-o! You itch all over and can't scratch yourself and you have to rub on this stuff that smells awful.
BILL: Maybe we can talk them into going someplace else for a change.

JANET: Like where?

BILL: Las Vegas.

JANET: Las Vegas?

BILL: Yeah. I see these commercials for it on TV all the time. Las Vegas looks hot with all kinds of neat stuff happening with music groups and gambling places that are all lit up. The place is a like this great big video game.

JANET: Mom'll never go for it.

BILL: How come?

JANET: Because it's not educational.

BILL: Hey! What's educational about watching people sleep in their chairs? Or make some stupid wooden bowl? But watching people gamble—that would be really interesting, I think.

JANET: Yeah. Watching some goon lose all his money would be really neat.

BILL: And they have all kinds of neat shows.

JANET: They wouldn't let us go. We'd have to have a babysitter or something and they'd get to go to all the shows and have all the fun.

BILL: Yeah, but during the day we'd get to hang out in the casinos and goof off and eat burgers and mess around while Mom and Dad gambled.

JANET: Mom gamble? Are you kidding? No way. And she won't go to Las Vegas, either. Forget it.

BILL: Nuts. I don't wanna go back to the Smoky Mountains again. I wanna go to Las Vegas where something's happening, you know.

JANET: Yeah, and where I wouldn't have to worry about getting poison ivy all the time.

MARY & CARL

Mary has difficulty convincing Carl that he should participate in her show.

MARY: Hey, Carl, I've been looking all over for you. I want you to be in my play.

CARL: A play? Gimme a break, okay? I hate plays. My mom made me go to this play once where a bunch of people were jumping around screaming and trying to be funny, but nobody laughed. Forget it.

MARY: But you'd be in this one. Like a big part in it, you know. Because I wrote it. It's a neat part. You get to be like this knight who like comes to town to kill this real bad dude who rips people off and steals their girlfriends. Your name is Sir Stanley.

CARL: What kind of a lame name is that?

MARY: Like a knight's name. They call knights "Sir." (*She forces at script on him.*) Here, read this. (*Pointing at the page.*) This part right here.

CARL: Bug off, okay? I'm not reading that kind of junk. I don't wanna be any Sir or anything, okay? I just wanna go home and watch TV.

MARY: Don't be dopey. It can't hurt you to at least try it, can it? I mean—

CARL Well—

MARY: can it? C'mon. (*Pointing to the page.*) Just this part right here where it says Sir Stanley. C'mon.

CARL: Well, okay. (*He takes the script and points to it.*) This part right here, right?

MARY: Yes—where it says Sir Stanley.

CARL: Why can't it be Sir Something Neat? Like—Sir Rambo, or something hot like that?

MARY: Because Sir Rambo would be dumb, that's why, spaz-o. C'mon, read it.

CARL: Okay, okay. (*He reads.*) "I have come to kill you, Henry, for robbing people and stealing their girlfriends and being a bad person. Prepare to die, you rat. He pulls out his sword."

MARY: No, no! you don't read that part.

CARL: It says right here, "He pulls out his sword."

MARY: That's like a direction, like to tell you what to do. That's the reason it's got a big red circle around it. Okay, go ahead—read after the part where you pull out your sword.

CARL: (*Reads.*) "This sword has killed a hundred dragons and many bad persons and now it is going to chop off your weasely head. He chops off his head."

MARY: No, no! That's another direction. You just act like you're chopping his head off. Okay, go ahead, start chopping.

CARL: (*Swinging his free arm in great, menacing arcs.*) "Take that, and that, and that, you mean, awful, terrible person."

MARY: All right! That was really cool.

CARL: It was? It was cool? Really, I mean, *really?*

MARY: Honest. The coolest, no kidding. You we're really great.

CARL: Wow.

MARY: You'll be a hit—a big star, Carl.

CARL: Then, hey, like don't call me Carl anymore, okay? Call me—Sir Stanley.

ELLEN & RICH

Younger brothers and sisters can be millstones.

ELLEN: Every time I go over to my grandparents, my sister wants to go along.

RICH: Yeah, the same with my little brother. I can't go anyplace without him always tagging along.

ELLEN: She always cries and goes crazy if they ask me to come over by myself.

RICH: My little brother started in kicking and screaming one time because I got to go with my dad to his office.

ELLEN: You know, sometimes I can't stand my sister because she acts like such a nerd.

RICH: When my brother comes along, nobody pays any attention to me because he's littler and they think he's cute.

ELLEN: Yeah, the same with me.

RICH: When he's there, it's like I'm not even around. I might as well be invisible. My brother makes me nervous, too. He never stops talking in this real loud, raspy voice, and he jumps around all the time and won't ever sit still. You know, sometime I think he's part monkey, or something.

ELLEN: The last time my sister went along to my grandparents, she crumbed crackers all over their living room and I got the blame. And then she went and trashed their kitchen and they all jumped on me for that, too. I mean, hey— gimme a break, okay?

RICH: Little kids can get away with all kinds of stuff. But if you're older, you can't get away with anything.

ELLEN: Sometimes I wish I was still little so I could mess up and be sloppy and yell around and always blame somebody else.

RICH: Do you have to watch your sister a lot?

ELLEN: All the time.

RICH: It's like I'm this babysitter, or something, you know.

ELLEN: Yeah—I've got plenty of more important stuff to do than watch out for some dorky little kid who won't listen to anything I tell her.

RICH: My brother gets into my toys and books and messes them up.

ELLEN: I think when I grow up, I'm not going to have any kids.

RICH: Me, either. I think I'll just have animals.

ELLEN: Me, too.

RICH: These people across the street from us don't have any kids. They just have two nice quiet dogs.

ELLEN: Animals don't yell and scream and act like jerks and get you in trouble and want to hang around you all the time.

RICH: I think brothers and sisters are a big waste of time—all of them.

ELLEN: Even the older ones. Like my big brother.

RICH: Yeah. They never want you to go anyplace with them or anything.

ELLEN: You know, I think it's the little kids and the big kids who are the real creeps.

ANNA & CLIVE

Divorce is a security-shattering experience.

ANNA: I heard about your mom and dad.

CLIVE: Who told you?

ANNA: Julie. She said that your father was living someplace else.

CLIVE: In an apartment, over on the West Side. I've been over there a bunch of times. He has an extra bedroom fixed up for me so I can stay over if I want to.

ANNA: My dad and mom got a divorce over a year ago. He lives in Phoenix now and is going to get married again.

CLIVE: We have our house up for sale.

ANNA: Wow!

CLIVE: And Mom's talking about moving back to her home town. It's this weird little place in Ohio with just one traffic light. My grandma and grandpa live there.

ANNA: I don't see my dad much anymore. Only on Sundays and holidays and stuff. It's seems real weird having him come to the house where he used to live.

CLIVE: At least you get to stay in your house and your own neighborhood. You're not moving. That way it isn't so scary, you know. And you'll still have the same friends and can go to the same school and everything.

ANNA: I know, I'm lucky I guess. But it still isn't like any fun without my dad living with us anymore.

CLIVE: It's weird.

ANNA: Sometimes I go to where he used to have his office in our house and I sit there and imagine he's still there messing with stuff at his desk and talking on the phone like always. I even talk to him.

CLIVE: You do?

ANNA: I tell him how much I miss him and how much I like him and how much I want him to come on back home.

CLIVE: It would be neat if people could always stay together and things would stay like they always were.

ANNA: A lot of kids' parents are getting divorced. A whole bunch.

CLIVE: How do people get so they don't like each other anymore?

ANNA: I don't know.

CLIVE: They did once, I guess.

ANNA: Yeah. I guess maybe something happens and they're not happy like they used to be.

CLIVE: When I ask Mom why Dad left, she never answers. She just looks off real sad or changes the subject or acts like she's busy.

ANNA: That's the reason I talk to my dad, even though he's not there.

CLIVE: How come?

ANNA: Because it's the only way I can get him to say anything.

BELINDA & CLARK

Tactfulness is easier to preach than practice.

BELINDA: Can I walk with you?

CLARK: If you want to.

BELINDA: I usually walk with Mary Ann Taylor, but she's got a cold and her voice sounds like a leaf blower.

CLARK: You kidding? Her voice always sounds like a leaf blower.

BELINDA: It does not!

CLARK: Like even worse. Like this big, raspy, loud noise like the sound a trash truck makes when it grinds up your garbage.

BELINDA: That's not nice. How would you like it if someone said something like that about you?

CLARK: It's the truth.

BELINDA: You can't always go around telling the truth.

CLARK: You think it's better to lie?

BELINDA: I don't mean you should lie, I mean like you should make the truth sound good so it doesn't hurt people's feelings, that's all.

CLARK: If someone's voice sounds like a jet plane, how can you tell them it does so it sounds good? You can't.

BELINDA: You can.

CLARK: Get real, okay?

BELINDA: You would say something like, "Hey, did anyone ever tell you have like this real strong but very interesting voice."

CLARK: That's stupid. How about, "Hey, gravel lungs, back off."

BELINDA: That's awful.

CLARK: It's better than what you said.

BELINDA: But what I said wouldn't make someone feel like a geek—it would be tactful.

CLARK: Yeah, but sometimes, when people are weird, you have to tell the honest truth because if you don't, they'll just keep on being weird. Like your shoes. They're kinda far out.

BELINDA: They are not, they're hot.

CLARK: Whatever you say.

BELINDA: What about your sweater? Where'd you get that hunk of junk, off a Goodwill truck?

CLARK: You don't like it?

BELINDA: It looks like somebody ran it through a paper shredder, that's what. Or maybe you stole it off the homeless. It's trash, it's awful, and I'll bet your dog sleeps in it because it stinks.

CLARK: Hey, Belinda.

BELINDA: I've never seen such an awful, ugly, dirty, cheap rag in my entire life.

CLARK: Hey!

BELINDA: And it's way too big and there are so many moth holes in it it looks like a fish net.

CLARK: (*Finally shouts.*) HEY! (*This stops her.*)

BELINDA: What?

CLARK: Gimme a break here, okay? Stop being so tactful.

DIANE & HOWARD

They discuss the passing of their father.

DIANE: Mom wants us to go to the funeral home again.
HOWARD: Do we have to?
DIANE: She wants us to. She said we should be there because it's like a good thing to do because we should all be together.
HOWARD: I think she needs us.
DIANE: I think so, too.
HOWARD: I don't like feeling sad, do you?
DIANE: Mom said it's okay to be sad, that being sad is good. She said that sometimes life is sad and sad things happen and that we should get used to it because it's part of growing up.
HOWARD: I think maybe growing up is hard.
DIANE: Me, too.
HOWARD: I never thought that people you liked a lot ever died.
DIANE: Me, neither, but they do. Everything dies sometime.
HOWARD: Mom said that crying is okay, too, because it makes you feel better because it lets you know more about what you feel inside.
DIANE: I guess sometimes before you can be happy again, you have to be sad.
HOWARD: I wish nobody ever died.
DIANE: Or ever left and went someplace else to live or ever stopped liking you.
HOWARD: I just wish Dad were still alive, that's all. And that we were still a family like always and everything was still the same.
DIANE: It's hard to think we'll never see him again.

HOWARD: Ernie Woodward's father died over a year ago and he said he still misses him a lot.

DIANE: Maybe you always do.

HOWARD: You think?

DIANE: Mom still talks about Grandma all the time; about the stuff they did and everything. She still misses her. And Grandpa does, too. He's always looking at her pictures and talking about when they were young and the things they used to do.

HOWARD: I wonder if I'll always be sad and feel like crying when I look in Dad's room and think back about all the stuff we did together?

DIANE: Maybe. But maybe after a while all of that goes away. The real sad part where you feel like crying all the time, I mean.

HOWARD: I sure hope so. I don't think I'd like feeling like this all the time—like sad and lonely, you know.

DIANE: Before Daddy died, he told us to be brave, remember?

HOWARD: And to look out for Mom.

DIANE: So we have to be brave like he wanted, okay?

HOWARD: Yeah. Maybe if we make him proud by being brave and taking care of Mom like he wanted, we won't have time to be sad for very long.

ESTHER & DARREN

It's difficult to meet parents' expectations.

DARREN: Most real smart kids I know seem to be like these spaced-out weirdos.

ESTHER: Who dress funny and sit around looking off into books all the time.

DARREN: Like Danny Richards.

ESTHER: Yeah. And Susan Goldman.

DARREN: They know everything.

ESTHER: Susan Goldman even knows about cave men and how they lived and how they invented fire.

DARREN: Big deal.

ESTHER: Yeah, but the teachers think she's neat.

DARREN: That's because when you know a whole lot of junk, it impresses older people and makes them think you're cool.

ESTHER: Even if you aren't.

DARREN: Danny Richards has this great big head, you ever notice?

ESTHER: I guess he has to have to keep all that junk he knows inside. You couldn't remember all that stuff with a regular head.

DARREN: You ever see the books he carries?

ESTHER: It's like he's carrying this library around under his arm.

DARREN: And he reads all that junk, too. Real fast. I saw him read a whole page in less than a minute one time. Like zap!

ESTHER: C'mon, nobody can read a page in a minute. It takes me a long time to read anything.

DARREN: Me, too.

ESTHER: Sue Goldman knows about poets and rattles off junk till it makes your eyes cross.

DARREN: It must be kinda neat being that smart, though, you know.

ESTHER: I guess. But she doesn't have any friends.

DARREN: Like Danny. His only friend is this real weird dude who talks like a grown-up person about politics and about what's going on in science. His name is Dave Ford. I was down in his basement one time and he's got like this thing set up with a zillion tubes and a whole bunch of electric stuff. Weird.

ESTHER: I wonder why sometimes when you're real smart, you don't have a bunch of friends?

DARREN: Because what can you say to them, you know. I mean, when I talk to Danny, it's like talking to this wizard or something.

ESTHER: Maybe they're smart because they don't goof off like the rest of us.

DARREN: How do you mean?

ESTHER: You know, like not paying attention and not doing our homework. Maybe we're just jealous.

DARREN: You think so?

ESTHER: Maybe being smart is more important than being popular.

DARREN: I don't know. Being popular is pretty neat.

ESTHER: Yeah but popular wears off and being smart doesn't.

DARREN: You know what? I never thought of that.

FRANCES & NORMAN

Dancing is not on Norman's agenda, but Sally Portman is.

NORMAN: Hey, Francis, where you going?

FRANCES: To dance class. I'm late.

NORMAN: I thought maybe we could go over to Kristin's house and watch videos.

FRANCES: I can't. Why don't you come along?

NORMAN: To dancing class? What for?

FRANCES: You can watch us practice ballet.

NORMAN: Are you kidding? Ballet? That'll be the day. When I hang around some lame place and watch a bunch of girls act like jerks. Ballet is stupid.

FRANCES: Oh yeah? Hey, we've got lots of boys in our class, too.

NORMAN: Sure. Like who, for instance?

FRANCES: Like Danny Rogers for instance.

NORMAN: Danny Rogers is a dork.

FRANCES: He is not! He's real graceful.

NORMAN: Maybe, but he's still a dork.

FRANCES: The one who's a dork is you.

NORMAN: Oh yeah?

FRANCES: It takes one to know one. Besides, he's a nice person.

NORMAN: You'll never catch me in one of those dopey outfits—no way!

FRANCES: You probably wouldn't be strong enough for ballet anyway. It'd be too hard for you.

NORMAN: Ballet? C'mon, do me a favor. What's so hard about walking around on your toes like a big, dumb geek?

FRANCES: It was too hard for Larry Johnson.

NORMAN: Larry Johnson was in your ballet class?

FRANCES: For almost a month.

NORMAN: He's one of the toughest dudes around.

FRANCES: He dropped out because he said it hurt him too much when he stretched and did jumps.

NORMAN: I still say ballet is for wimps.

FRANCES: Just because you think it is doesn't make it so. Lots of boys take tap and jazz and ballet and everything. In fact, Ms. Adams, our teacher, she said a whole bunch of your big sports stars do ballet to make them stronger and help them to move better.

NORMAN: Who else is in your class?

FRANCES: Sue Reed and Julie Hartman and Mindy White and Sally Portman, and—

NORMAN: (*Overlapping.*) Sally Portman? She's in your class?

FRANCES: She's really good, too, she can—

NORMAN: (*Overlapping.*) Sally Portman who lives over on Cedar Street? Man, she's cool! She's in your ballet class?

FRANCES: Yes.

NORMAN: Wow! Say, you know what? Maybe I will come along after all. Not to dance or anything like that, just to hang around and watch and stuff.

FRANCES: I thought you said ballet was stupid.

NORMAN: (*His voice trails off as they exit.*) I didn't say ballet was stupid. Do you know that a lot of your top sports guys take ballet to get in shape and get stronger and stuff? Ballet is cool, ballet is—

WILMA & PAUL

A discussion regarding diet.

WILMA: Yuck! How can you eat that junk?

PAUL: Hey, get off my back, okay?

WILMA: That kind of food is full of salt and grease and all kinds of junk. My mother says that kids shouldn't eat burgers and fries and shakes and stuff because it's junk food and it makes you fat.

PAUL: Hey. You know what? Just because all you brought along is a banana, you want everybody else to starve to death, too.

WILMA: Bananas are good for you, everybody knows that. And they're not fattening.

PAUL: And they haven't got any flavor, either.

WILMA: You keep eating that junk and you'll turn into a fat slob.

PAUL: And if you keep hogging down bananas, you're gonna wind up looking like an ape.

WILMA: I am not an ape!

PAUL: You will be if you keep eating jungle food. You ever go to the zoo?

WILMA: Sure, lots of times.

PAUL: Okay, monster brain, how about what they feed the animals. Bananas and fruit and junk. And look at them. They all look sad and mangy.

WILMA: That's because they're caged up.

PAUL: Uh uh, it's because they keep stuffing them full of fruit. I'll bet if they gave them burgers they'd look better in no time.

WILMA: Apes wouldn't eat burgers.

PAUL: How do you know?

WILMA: You're stupid.

PAUL: If I was stupid, I'd be eating a banana.

WILMA: You just wait and see. When you grow up, you're going to be big and fat and then you'll be sorry you ate all kinds of junk when you were a kid.

PAUL: My aunt eats fruit all the time, and all kinds of health stuff, too. My dad calls it bird food. And she's as big as a truck. When she gets into our car, one whole side of it goes down.

WILMA: You can't get fat from eating bananas.

PAUL: If you eat a whole bunch you can.

WILMA: Nobody eats a whole bunch, lame-o.

PAUL: Except apes and they look awful.

WILMA: I'm not going to sit by you anymore.

PAUL: How come?

WILMA: Because your fingers are all greasy.

PAUL: At least my mouth's not full of a glob of bananas that looks like ape barf.

WILMA: Apes. All you think about is apes.

PAUL: You want a bite of my Quarter Pounder?

WILMA: No way.

PAUL: You know, maybe that's the good thing about us sitting together.

WILMA: What's that?

PAUL: That you'll never have to worry about me wanting one of your bananas, and I'll never have to worry about you eating up my fries.

YOLANDA & ZACK

Yolanda and Zack express concern for the less fortunate, and realize the joy of giving.

YOLANDA: Do you know what? Sometimes, when I'm in bed at night, I think about how it would be not to have a nice warm house and friends and food and nice clothes and everything.

ZACK: And a nice family and lots of toys and TV. Come to think of it, we're really lucky, you know that?

YOLANDA: This Christmas, I'm not asking for a whole bunch of stuff like always.

ZACK: Me, neither.

YOLANDA: Even though I like toys, I don't think getting a whole bunch of new stuff just because it's new is a very good idea. My closet's already so full of toys and clothes and junk you can't get anything else in it. When my father looks at it, he just shakes his head. He can't believe it, I guess.

ZACK: A whole bunch of my stuff is piled up out in the garage because there isn't any more room for it in the house.

YOLANDA: Really? The same with me.

ZACK: Know what I'm going to do? This year, I'm going to box it all up and give it to kids who don't have as much as me.

YOLANDA: Yeah, me, too. That's a good idea. You know Cindy Riley, don't you?

ZACK: Yeah.

YOLANDA: Well, the other day I went over to her house to play. She doesn't have much because her father left and her mother has to work at the department store. I'll bet she didn't have more than two dolls. But you know, even though Cindy didn't have a bunch of toys, it didn't seem to make any difference. She seemed to be more happy than a lot of kids I know whose parents are rich.

ZACK: I know her older brother, Charles. He's a real nice kid who works over at the grocery after school.

YOLANDA: When Mom and I were downtown last Saturday, we saw all these people hanging around on the street. They looked all grubby and tired.

ZACK: That's because they don't have anyplace to go. They have to hang around outside in all kinds of weather and sleep in the parks and stuff.

YOLANDA: Mom said that we should always be really grateful for all the nice things we have and that we should understand that a lot of people in the world don't and that many of them are hungry and afraid.

ZACK: Someday, when I get old enough, I'm going try to help out poor people.

YOLANDA: The other day, I told Cindy I'd give her some of my old toys. And it made me feel really neat inside. Like even better than when I get stuff myself.

ZACK: I guess that's because giving stuff is the best gift of all.